My Animal abc

by
RENE CLOKE

a

airplane

antelope

axe

ape

apple

b

balloon

bear

bell

butterfly

book

badger

ball

C cherries

cow

cat

camera

camel

cap

d

donkey

drum

doll

duck

dog

e

eagle

elephant

egg

engine

f

foxglove

fox

frog

fan

fish

goat

g

grasshopper

goose

gate

h

house

hat

hen

horse

harp

i

indian

ice cream

iron

ink

j

jack-
in-
a-box

jug

jam

jay

k

kite

kitten

kettle

kangaroo

m

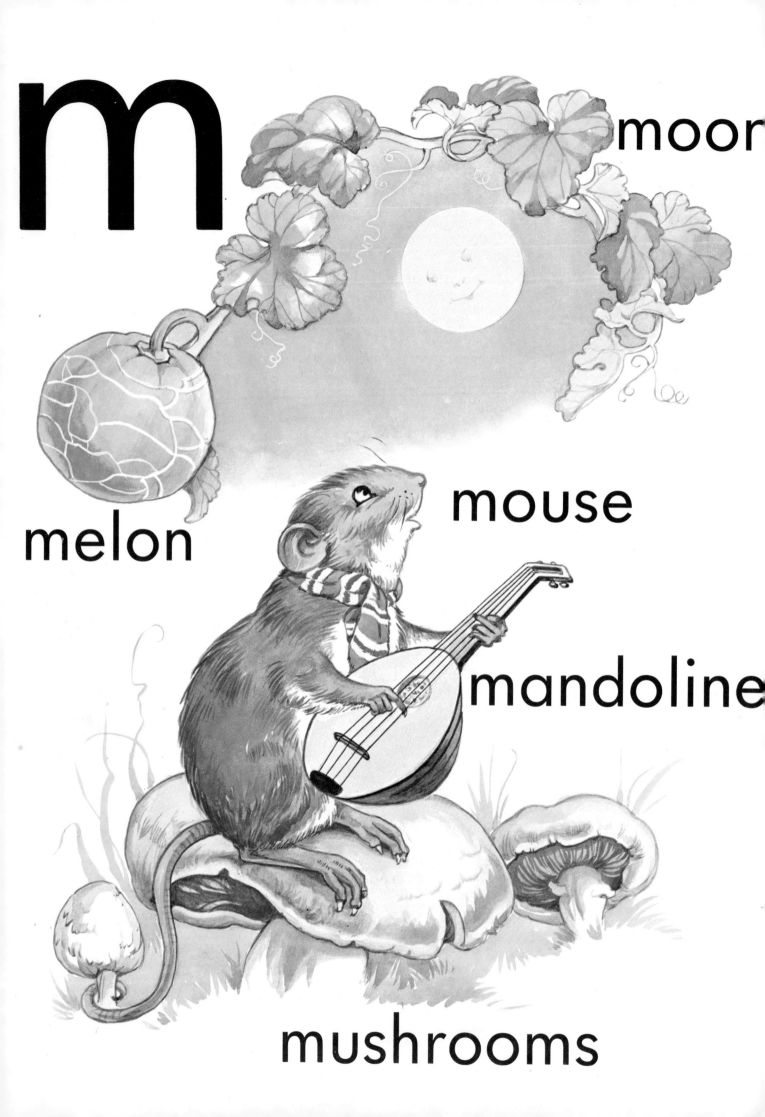

moon

melon

mouse

mandoline

mushrooms

n

net

nail

nutcracker

nut

newt

O

owl

orange

ostrich

otter

p

parrot

picture

porcupine

pig

pencil

paintbox

q

queen

quilt

quail

r

rose

rake

rabbit

robin

raspberries

S

star

soldier

stag

squirrel

snail

strawberries

t

teddy bear

tree

tiger

turtle

teapot

U

umbrella

unicorn

V

van

vulture

violin

vole

violets

W

windmill

witch

wheelbarrow

wolf

X

xylophone

y

yellowhammer

yew tree

yak

yacht

z

ZOO

zoo

zebra   zinnias